A BOOT UP

NORTH DEVON

Rosanna Rothery

HALSGROVE

First published in Great Britain in 2008

Copyright © 2008 Text: Rosanna Rothery
Photographs: Jon Bowen

Front cover: Looking towards Lee Bay from Ilfracombe.

British Library Cataloguing-in-Publication Data
A CIP record for this title is available from the British Library

ISBN 978 1 84114 828 1

Halsgrove House
Ryelands Industrial Estate, Bagley Road,
Wellington, Somerset TA21 9PZ
Tel: 01823 653777
Fax: 01823 216796
email: sales@halsgrove.com
website: www.halsgrove.com

Printed and bound by D'Auria Industrie Grafiche, Italy

Contents

	Introduction	4
1	**Hartland**	7
2	**Clovelly**	13
3	**Lynmouth**	19
4	**Lee Bay**	25
5	**Saunton**	31
6	**Mortehoe**	35
7	**Arlington**	41
8	**Combe Martin**	47
9	**Weare Giffard**	53
10	**Baggy Point**	59

Introduction

Here are ten exciting, varied and beautiful days out in the North Devon countryside. You will be struck by the phenomenal contrasts in scenery in this remarkably unspoilt corner of the county.

To indulge a traditional image of Devon that consists of thatched cottages, cream teas, window boxes and pretty fishing villages this book takes you to the cobbled streets of picture postcard pretty Clovelly as well as to the quaint thatched roof tops of Weare Giffard and Lee.

However, if you wish to take a walk on the wild side, the savage scenery encountered on a rocky ramble around Morte Point won't disappoint nor will romantic windswept roams around Baggy Point and Hartland Quay.

For a different perspective on North Devon, be bowled over by the beautiful panoramas atop some of the UK's highest cliffs at Combe Martin or on a high coastal trek from Ilfracombe towards Lee Bay. To wonder at wildlife or peruse wild plants then a stroll through the North Devon Biosphere Reserve at Braunton Burrows is a must as is a visit to the hide and lake at Arlington Court.

For swimmers, surfers and sunbathers this region boasts some of the best beaches in the country, from the surf

Meccas of Croyde and Woolacombe to the long stretch of Saunton Sands.

Lovers of literature and history are not left out either. Take a peek at Blackpool Mill cottage, which featured in the BBC's adaptation of *Sense and Sensibility*, visit the fictional birth-place of Tarka The Otter and discover more about the eccentric former owner of Arlington Court.

Finally, for tranquillity nothing quite compares with the cascading beauty of rivers tumbling over boulders – the gorges at Watersmeet, near Lynmouth, are exceptionally peaceful.

All these routes can be extremely muddy and good walking shoes and waterproofs are essential. None are

pushchair friendly so toddlers need to be backpacked.

Circular routes follow public rights of way or access land, which were accu-rate at the time of going to press but can be subject to change or diversion, so do always take a map with you, especially if you plan to make detours or go off route. Two Ordnance Survey maps cover all the walks which are

accessible by car: OS Landranger 180 Barnstaple and Ilfracombe or OS Landranger 190 Bude and Clovelly.

Mileage has been worked out using a global positioning system. The timings given are the walking time only – they don't include stops for picnics, rests, visits to the pub, photographs etc, so remember to take account of these when planning your day.

Key to Symbols Used

Level of difficulty:

Easy 🥾

Moderate 🥾 🥾

More challenging 🥾 🥾 🥾

Map symbols:

🚗   Park & start

▭▭▭▭   Tarred Road

‑ ‑ ‑   Unpaved road

– – –   Footpath

■   Building

+   Church

▲   Triangulation pillar or other landmark

🚻   WC

🍴   Refreshments

🍺   Pub

Walk Locations

Lee Bay

Morte Point ⑥ ④ ■ Ilfracombe ⑧ ■ ③ Lynton

Combe Martin
A39

Lundy Island

A3123

Baggy Point ⑩ Croyde

N
W ✦ E
S

⑦ Arlington A399

Saunton ⑤ A39

Braunton
■ A361

■ Barnstaple

■ Bideford

② Clovelly
A39

A361

⑨ Weare Giffard

① ■ Hartland

■ Torrington

To M5

Hartland Quay

1 Hartland

A 5 mile coastal walk taking you past the 15th century cottage and the dramatic pebble beach where the 2008 BBC adaptation of *Sense and Sensibility* was filmed.

Ever since Edward Ferrars proposed to Elinor Dashwood at a tiny cottage on a rugged and romantic clifftop, visitors have flocked in their thousands to this dramatic and windswept stretch of the North Devon coast. In 2007, Blackpool Mill cottage, part of the Hartland Abbey Estate, became the setting for a BBC adaptation of Jane Austin's *Sense and Sensibility*, a film which fired the nation's romantic pulse on New Year's Day 2008. This stunning walk takes you past the 15th century cottage, which in the three-part adaptation by scriptwriter Andrew Davies, became Barton Cottage. Those captivated by Austin's powerful and passionate tale will certainly recognise the cosy little house where Mrs Dashwood lived with her three daughters, and its sensationally beautiful clifftop setting.

Length: 5 miles
Time: 2 hours 30 mins
Level: 🐾 🐾 Moderate. There are a couple of steep cliff climbs.

Directions to get there: From Bideford take the A39 towards Bude and turn right when you see signs for Hartland (B3248). Follow the signs to Stoke and park near St Nectan's Church.
OS Map: Landranger 190 Bude and Clovelly
Start and park: SS 23506 24709
Refreshments: For bar meals there is the Hartland Quay Hotel (01237 441218). Stoke Barton Farm (01237 441238) does a superb cream tea in the holiday season and Hartland Abbey serves light lunches and cream teas in the warmer months (phone for admission prices and opening times: 01237 441264).

This coastal route also takes in the rocky cove of Hartland Quay with its imposing furrowed cliffs and the splashing waterfall of Speke's Mill Mouth, passing striking rock formations along the way.

ATLANTIC OCEAN

Hartland Quay 🍴 🚻

St Catherine's Point

Tower

ke's Mill

Wargery Farm

Stoke 🍴 🚻

To Hartland

1 The walk begins at St Nectan's Church, where from lofty heights, a set of grimacing gargoyles appear to send you on your way. The church's commanding 128 feet tower, claimed to be the highest in Devon, can be seen for miles from all directions and has long been used as a landmark by ships at sea. Little wonder this church, the glory of Stoke, is often referred to as the Cathedral of North Devon. In Medieval times, it is said, monks from Hartland Abbey would make the uphill pilgrimage to the church, half a dozen times, both day and night. Even if you are not quite that dedicated to religious duties, it's still worth a look inside.

Begin walking along the road, with St Nectan's Church on your right, until

St Nectan's Church tower

you come to a public footpath sign directing you into a field. The path curves around the right-hand edge and then the bottom of the field with a stream to your right.

2 In the far corner, the path takes you into woodland. Trees arch magnificently over this track as you wend your way through

the valley. Occasionally you may find yourself having to bend to get beneath branches which, over the ages, have fused into extraordinary tangles. This gnarly valley is famous for its snowdrops in early spring,

The Hartland Abbey Estate is a popular film location due to its mix of medieval, Georgian, Regency, Victorian and Gothic influences.

Gnarled tree, Hartland

which are soon replaced by a blanket of bluebells and other wild flowers in the warmer months.

3 When you see a pretty bridge across the river take a left, signposted: Hartland Quay 1 mile. Pass through the wooden gate. If you look to your right you will see the little holiday home which became Barton Cottage in the BBC's adaptation of *Sense and Sensibility*. Listen to the sea ripple across the stones on the shoreline and you'll appreciate just why the film's location manager chose this romantic cove as a setting. From

Blackpool Mill cottage, Hartland

here the path takes you up. Look back for sweeping views over the bay. It is quite a steep climb but worth it for the views at the top. It's a sheer drop over the edge, on your right.

4 The path eventually draws parallel with a tower, which directly lines up with the Abbey behind it. You are now on the top of Hartland Quay. Continue walking with the sea to your right.

Rock formations near Hartland Quay

St Catherine's Tor on the walk from Hartland Quay

5 The path leads you to a gate. Go through and turn right. You are now heading down the hill via the road. (For a shorter walk you can always turn left and follow the road back to Stoke – see the OS map).

6 If you want to make an interesting detour continue down this road to Hartland Quay.

During the filming of Sense and Sensibility in May 2007, visitors to Hartland Abbey frequently encountered actors and actresses in period costume wandering around the house and gardens.

Here furrowed cliffs form a breathtaking backdrop to a boulder-strewn beach. To continue, pick up the coastal path in the top car park signposted: Speke's Mill 1 mile. Keep to the lowest path which passes a series of incredible rock formations with the sea to your right. Eventually you encounter the strange protuberance of St Catherine's Point, a coastal tor that looks like it has been sliced in two – you can even examine the rocky ridges in the cross section. The path passes behind the point and, depending on how rainy it has been, you might find yourself crossing a little stream via stepping stones. The path takes you across a flat field before once again climbing up the sea cliffs. It then drops down onto a stony path which eventually becomes proper

steps leading down to Speke's Mill Mouth. Here a stream tumbles over the edge of the cliff into a pretty waterfall. You might like to take a detour and climb down to the beach – a good place for a picnic.

7 To continue, take a left onto the path which starts to take you inland. You will pass a signpost for Lymebridge ¾ of a mile. At the fork take the right hand path. It passes through a metal gate over a

Tower at Hartland

cattle grid. The path eventually comes out on a road. Take a left.

8 Take another left at Speke's Valley Cottage. The stream is to your right as you climb this road.

9 At Kernstone Cross go straight over onto a road marked: Unsuitable For Motors. At Wargery Farm the path swings to the left and you can see the tower of St Nectan's ahead.

View south from Hartland Quay

View out to sea near Hartland Quay

10 When you arrive back in Stoke, follow the road around to the left. It will take you past Stoke Barton Farm where Helen Davey will defy you to manage an entire cream tea by yourself. The road leads you back to your car. A visit to historical Hartland Abbey on your way home is recommended.

Blackpool Mill cottage had a clever transformation at the hands of the BBC's set design team, who added a porch, a pebbled and shelled front garden and a lick of paint.

2 Clovelly

A superb coastal 7.7 mile walk that leads you to the quaint cobbled fishing village of Clovelly.

The little fishing village of Clovelly, it has been said, has been featured on more calendars than any other village in the UK. With colourful window boxes, cobbled streets and whitewashed cottages clinging to a steep ravine that leads down to the sea, there can be few places as picturesque. Yet beneath the chocolate box charm, there's evidence that residents have to be pretty hardy to live in this working fishing village. For a start no cars are allowed. That means the village's preposterously steep cobbles have to be negotiated every time residents want to go anywhere and, to carry shopping up and down the streets, they are obliged to use sledges.

In days gone by residents must have been pretty robust too – the coastline was rife with smuggling, wrecking and piracy. For today's visitor there are less treacherous attractions as you will discover on this fabulous coastal

Length: 7.7 miles

Time: 2 hours 45 mins

Level: 🐾 🐾 Moderate. The climb up through the cobbled streets of Clovelly is challenging.

Directions to get there: Take the A39 from Bideford. Turn right onto the B3248 and then left. Stay on the road until you reach Brownsham. Park in the car park.

OS Map: OS Landranger 190 Bude and Clovelly

Start and park: SS 28500 25900

Refreshments: The Red Lion Pub (01237 431237) on Clovelly harbour serves bar snacks at lunchtime and evenings from 6pm. It is also open for three course evening meals. There are plenty of eateries in the village.

Note: Paths can be muddy and the cobbled Clovelly streets are steep – suitable footwear is essential.

walk which takes you through the heart of the charming old fishing village.

TLANTIC
OCEAN

Mouthmill Beach
Blackchurch Rock

Brownsham

Clovelly Court

Clovelly

B3237

1 The route begins on a little path which leads you out of the back of the Brownsham Car Park signposted: Beckland Woods. You will soon pass through a small wooden gate which takes you into the woods. After a gate turn right onto a path signposted: Woodland Walk Coast Path. Keep following the signs through the wood to the coast path. The path takes you along the bottom of fields which have sweeping views across to Baggy Point.

2 Climb over the stile signposted: Mouthmill. You are now high above the sea. Take a glance back for a spectacular view of Lundy Island. The path leads you across a field which boasts spectacular views of the coast and neighbouring headlands Baggy Point and Morte Point. Keep following the signs to Mouthmill.

3 The path descends into woodland. Be prepared for a long descent.

4 At the end of the wood turn left onto the path signposted: Coast Path. This path leads you down to the blustery cove of Mouthmill Beach, distinctive for its old lime Kiln and the impressive twin tunnels of the sea-smacked Blackchurch Rock. Walk across the boulders and pick up the path by the big stone wall on the far

Blackchurch Rock

Clovelly has no cars and no individually-owned houses. It is owned by one family (one of only three since the Norman Conquest).

side of the beach. The path ascends into Brownsham Woods. Follow the coast path signs leading you up through woodland and gorse.

(5) Eventually you come across a pretty carved bench, a lovely viewing point and a great place for a picnic. Continue to follow the coastal path.

(6) The path continues through woods before taking you into a field. You're now skirting the grounds of Clovelly Court. The path soon leads you through a kissing gate into a little wooded area and out the other side. Stay on this coastal track which eventually ends at a big black metal gate.

(7) On the other side of the gate turn left and walk down the road to the bottom of the steep hill. Passing through the arch of the Red Lion Hotel, you will find yourself on Clovelly Harbour. Do take a while to sit on the quay and indulge in freshly caught fish sold here during the

Coast path to Clovelly

Charles Kingsley lived in Clovelly as a child and returned many times as an adult, staying at what is known as Kingsley Cottage.

warmer months. Take in the pretty little village and harbour with its curving breakwater, boats at anchor and fishermen's nets. If you're feeling particularly maudlin you might like to contemplate the fate of poor old Crazy Kate. Her cottage, one of the oldest in

Boats in Clovelly Harbour

the village, is directly opposite. Kate Lyall died in 1736. She used to watch and wait from her upper window for her husband, who fished in the bay. One day a storm blew up just outside the harbour and tragically Kate watched her husband meet his watery demise. Losing her mind, she donned her wedding dress and waded into the sea to join him.

8 From the harbour the only way is up – pick up the cobbled path by the Red Lion Hotel. There are plenty of places to visit on the way to the top including the Kingsley Museum, celebrating the life of Victorian author Charles Kingsley, and an old fisherman's cottage showing how a Clovelly family would have lived in the 1930s.

Cobbled Clovelly street

9 At the top take a right, opposite the old police station, and stay on the road until you come to Clovelly Court Garden.

10 Take a right into the stately drive and walk down to the house. Here turn left signposted: Court Farm, Sawmills. Follow this lane down into a wooded area. Ignore signs to the coast path. Instead stay on this lane which is marked by public bridleway signs. You pass a house on your right and you go past some farm buildings before the path becomes a track between fields with fences on either side. Continue with trees to your right and a hedge to your left. It can be extremely muddy.

(11) When you get to the field do not stay on the path but instead aim towards a solitary gate in the middle. The grassy path that takes you there is not always distinct. The gate, which at the time of writing was not attached to any fence, has a blue public bridleway sign on it. Now head for the wooden gate directly opposite, which again is marked by a blue sign. Follow the hedge on your right and you'll come to the next blue arrow leading you down into the woods.

Red Lion Hotel, Clovelly

Charles Kingsley wrote Westward Ho! while in Clovelly and the village also inspired him to write The Water Babies.

Clovelly village from the harbour

12 Go through a metal gate and continue down the rocky path. When this comes out onto another path take a left. Take the next right and the path takes you across a stream. Then take the next left which is a steady climb through the woods to Brownsham.

13 At the top of the wood you will come to a cluster of cottages on your right. Take a left out onto the road. You will soon come to the car park on your right.

Clovelly's famous cobbled street, known as Up Along or Down Along, was built from pebbles hauled from the beach.

Above: Clovelly beach

Below: The top end of Clovelly

3 Lynmouth

A 4.7 mile relaxing riverside walk in a wooded valley following deep river gorges and fast-flowing waters.

Ah the bliss of tranquillity. There is something incredibly soothing about walking beside a cascading river beneath a canopy of ancient woodland. On this walk you will find yourself strolling beneath a green awning of oak, ash and wych elm while listening to the mesmerising sound of gushing waters tumbling over huge boulders. It instills a sense of peacefulness even when there are swarms of visitors around (as is quite likely in the summer months).

At Watersmeet you will want to while away a few moments and listen to the cacophony of two rivers merging into each other's flow – Hoar Oak Water and East Lyn. The plunging sprays of water are quite stunning. This magical route also takes in aerial views of the river and the twin villages of Lynton and Lynmouth.

Length: 4.7 miles

Time: 2 hours

Level: 👢 👢 👢 👢 Hard due to one steep climb. However there is an easy flat alternative route included at marker four where you can retrace your steps along the river.

Directions to get there: From Barnstaple follow the A39 to Lynmouth and Lyndale Car Park is on your right when you get to the village.

OS Map: OS Landranger 180 Barnstaple and Ilfracombe

Start and park: SS 72434 49422

Refreshments: This walk leads you to Watersmeet House, a National Trust tea shop. From March until the beginning of November it opens at 10.30am and serves snacks. Half way around this walk, is the Blue Ball Inn. Traditional pub food is served all day during the warmer months (except between 4pm and 5pm). For details ring: 01598 741263. There are plenty of restaurants and tea shops in Lynton and Lynmouth.

Notes: When in spate the river should be respected. Take care near the water and on slippery rocks and paths.

ATLANTIC OCEAN

Lynmouth

Countisbury Hill

Blue Ball Pub 🍺 🍴 🚻 6

Lynton 🚗 1

River West Lyn

9 8 7 5

Myrtleberry House

River East Lyn 4

2

Watersmeet Road 3

National Trust Teahouse 🍴 🚻

Sadly such peaceful tranquillity seems a long way from the tragic events of August 15, 1952 when, after an exceptionally wet early August, nine inches of rain fell in 24 hours.

1 Our walk begins from the Lyndale Car Park where you need to turn right at the paying kiosk. You are now on a narrow path with the river flowing to your left. Cross the

Plunging spray at Watersmeet

bridge and, on the other side, take a right. You'll pass a row of pretty coast guard cottages to your left. Soon the tarmac road becomes a riverside path where fast flowing waters tumble over rocks to your right. Ignore the first wooden bridge and continue along the path. You are now in a photographer's paradise. It is not unusual to spot a jay, wood warbler or sparrowhawk as you follow the path along these fabulous, deep gorges. We are told that otters have returned to the more secluded parts of the river and, if you are very lucky you might spot red deer in among the trees. As for the sound, the roar of waters is both exhilarating and relaxing. After a while you'll pass a signpost: Watersmeet Countisbury. Continue along the riverside path.

River at Watersmeet

2 At the fork take the right-hand path signposted: Watersmeet Riverside Walk. Soon Blackpool Bridge, a wooden arch over the river takes you over rushing waters. On the other side, the path continues to your left. After a steady climb you come to a signpost: Footpath Watersmeet. Continue along the path next to the river.

Ignore the next bridge and continue towards Watersmeet. Soon to your

The Rising Sun at Lynmouth

Path to Countisbury

right you will see the site of the former Lynrock Water Factory (look out for a ginger beer bottle in the wall). The path curves around to the right, past the private residence of Myrtleberry House. Pass by the impressive stone arch of Chiselcombe Bridge and continue on the path.

3 At the fork take a left down to the wooden bridge. You will want to spend a while here looking at the magnificent waterfall. If you are extremely lucky, you might see a proud-necked heron intermittently make hungry snaps at a leaping salmon — the fish being determined to jump the river's shoots and rapids. On the other side of the bridge, turn left and cross over another bridge which leads you to a former fishing lodge, now Watersmeet House, where you can buy refreshments and contemplate the beauty around you.

4 Follow the path around the bottom of the tea shop gardens with the river to your left. At the fork take a right. The path is sign-

National Trust Teahouse, Watersmeet

posted: Lynmouth. Walk past Chiselcombe Bridge again, which is now on your left. If you want an easier flatter walk back, then cross the bridge and retrace your steps back to the car park. To continue, follow the path signposted: Woodland Walk Lynmouth. It climbs then drops to a stone wall. Continue along with the wall to your left, shaded by woods.

 5 After a low stone wall take a right signposted: Footpath to Countisbury. This is a long hard rocky climb. The path passes through a small wooden gate and continues up through the middle of a steep valley towards the road. Don't forget to glance back for views.

6 If climbing to the top of the valley leaves you exhausted make a detour to the road and the Blue Ball Inn. To continue walking though, you need to take a left at the top of the path signposted: Lynmouth. Cross the top of the valley and turn left, away from the road. You can see the path in front of you forming a ridge around the top of the valley.

Watersmeet

Follow the signposts to Lynmouth. Stunning views along this valley-top ridge will make the recent strenuous climb seem worthwhile. The path passes through a wooden gate and then begins to drop down.

7 At the fork where there is a wooden bench take a right signposted: Lynmouth Via Beacon Tor. The path curves around past a beautiful stone wall before continuing to wind up and down. After a while you will witness stunning aerial views of

Autumn colours, Lynmouth

As a result of the 1952 floods, lessons were learned about the bridges – the present Lynrock Bridge is designed to float away in the event of serious flooding while Chiselcombe Bridge, opened in 1957, is much higher than its predecessors.

Lynton and Lynmouth (the Little Switzerland of North Devon) and the East Lyn River.

8 At a signpost called Sparrow's Walk take a left down the hill signposted: Lynmouth via Sparrow's Walk. The path zigzags down through the trees.

9 At the bottom turn right and then left over the bridge. At the other side of the bridge turn right and take the path which takes you along the river and back to the car park on your left.

Aerial view, Lynmouth

4 Lee Bay

A varied 9.3 mile circular from Ilfracombe to the pretty village of Lee taking in superb coastal views, ancient woodland, a nature reserve and the Slade Reservoirs.

This coastal route leads you away from the tourist trap of Ilfracombe towards the tranquillity of Lee, a village surrounded by thickly wooded hills, lush meadows, sparkling streams, a rocky cove and rugged cliffs. It's a walk that really does have have everything – from astonishing cliff-top panoramas, including stunning aerial perspectives of Ilfracombe, to the secluded rocky cove of Lee Bay. You'll discover the pretty village of Lee, ancient woods, the Old Railway line, Slade Reservoirs and Cairn Nature Reserve.

Length: 9.3 miles

Time: 3 hours 11 mins

Level: 🐾 🐾 🐾 A long walk.

Directions to get there: From Barnstaple take the A361 to Ilfracombe. Take a left into Wilder Road and you will come to Bath Place Car Park on your left.

OS Map: OS Landranger 180 Barnstaple and Ilfracombe

Start and park: SS 51542 47682

Refreshments: The Grampus Inn (01271 862906) in Lee serves lunches, evening meals from 7pm and afternoon cream teas. Ilfracombe has a good variety of eateries.

Cliffs near Ilfracombe

Coastal view from Ilfracombe

(1) Bath Place Car Park is directly opposite Ilfracombe's oldest tourist attraction, The Tunnels Beaches. Take the road next to the Tunnels Beaches Bath House, called Torrs Park. Turn right into Granville Road and a signpost directs you to the public footpath. Go left at Torrs Walk Avenue and, at the end of the private road, just after the Avoncourt Hotel, take a right. Follow the path which becomes a narrow track leading you around the back of the houses. Turn right at the National Trust Torrs Walk sign.

Often referred to locally as Fuchsia Valley, during the flowering months, Lee's pretty hedgerows are famous for the vibrant blooms.

(2) At the first fork take a left. The path climbs in a zigzag fashion for some while. On a clear day you'll see Wales.

(3) The path passes through a small wooden gate. Here to your right you'll see a viewing point – a perfect spot for a picnic. From the top, looking out to sea, enjoy stunning aerial views of Ilfracombe to your right, and a beauty parade of headlands to your left.

To continue return to the wooden gate and turn left following the path as it curves around to your right. Follow it down along the hedge to the stile. Go across a grassy area with the sea to your right. After a while the path narrows before taking you across more grassland.

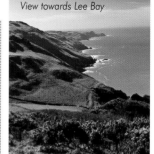

View towards Lee Bay

(4) Go over the stile. At this fork go right following the signpost to Lee. A corrugated stone path leads you up again before opening out and taking you across more grassland. The path narrows by some gorse and then descends following a hedge. Go through the gate and enjoy an incredibly steep descent to Lee Bay. At the bottom of the lane turn right onto the road.

Southcliffe Hall, Lee

Southcliffe Hall is the former residence of Rev George Tugwell, the first vicar of Lee, a keen naturalist and friend of the author George Eliot who visited the village in 1856.

path sign, climb over a stile on your right just before Southcliffe Hall. Follow the path across the grass to a stile by a stream. Go over the footbridge and turn left. The path, which can be extremely muddy, follows the stream. Eventually you come to a stile. Climb over and continue.

Turn left at the signpost: Public Footpath to Shaftsborough. Then go left again over a little bridge. On the other side of the bridge take a left

 Soon you arrive at Lee Bay beach, a former smugglers' haunt for the likes of six foot, long haired, Cruel Coppinger's gang member, Hannibal Richards. Continue along the road and take a left signposted: Footpath to Lee Village. (You

pick up this footpath to the right of the car park). To make a detour follow this path to the Grampus Inn and pretty Lee village.

To continue, however, halfway up the path, at a public foot-

Lee Bay

Borough Woods, near Lee

signposted: Public Footpath. This path climbs up.

7 When the path meets a track go right (not up the steps opposite). This track, passing through recent conifer plantations, eventually combines with another track. At this fork go right. The path ascends until eventually you reach a metal gate.

8 At the road turn right and at Mallards Corner take a right over Lee Bridge. Take the next right

into the layby. At the bottom of the layby turn right onto the Old Railway Line, passing under a bridge.

This lovely straight path into Ilfracombe passes Slade Reservoirs to your left — look out for kingfishers, deer and otters. Eventually you'll go through Cairn Nature Reserve, home to woodpeckers, jays, tawny owls, foxes, badgers and adders. Keep your eye open for a phantom bunny as apparently the ghost of a Jewish peddler, reportedly murdered on Cairn Top in the 1790s, still roams here in rabbit form.

9 At the end of the two mile trail, with the Pall factory to your left, follow the road downhill through Lamb Park. Pass Ilfracombe

A small cave above Sandy Cove, just west of Lee Bay, was a hang-out for smuggler Hannibal Richards and it was to here that he would escape when his gang was raided by the revenue men.

Parish Church on your left and take the second left at the roundabout into Wilder Road. Continue until you see the car park on your left.

Lee Bay

5 Saunton

An all-day 9.5 mile beach walk leading you through the mighty sand-hills of Braunton Burrows and along the glorious stretch of Saunton Sands.

This lovely long beach walk, which takes in the great golden expanse of Saunton Sands, is worth making a day of. Pack a picnic — even a swimming costume if you fancy a dip.

Braunton Burrows is a magical place and provides a superb spot for snoozing or lazing about in the sun — especially if there is a breeze coming off the sea. A mere stone's throw away the beach might be heaving but, in one of these sheltered cozy hollows, you can doze off in solitude.

This is a lengthy walk but, along the way, there are places to sit and relax surrounded by contrasting scenes of dunes, mud-

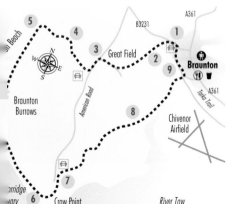

Length: 9.5 miles
Time: 3 hours 15 mins
Level: 🐾 🐾 🐾 A little hard. This is a long walk but there are plenty of places to stop along the way.
Directions to get there: Take the A361 to Braunton and the Caen Car Park is on the B3231 Saunton Road.
OS Map: OS Landranger 180 Barnstaple and Ilfracombe
Start and park: SS 48707 36539
Refreshments: If you work up an appetite for a fishy feast, Squires Fish Restaurant (01271 815533) in Braunton is a celebrated chippie which also has a takeaway.
Note: Strong currents in the river at Crow Point make it unsuitable for swimming.

flats, sand, sea and the Taw and Torridge Estuary.

1 From Caen Car Park, go out to the main road and take a left along Saunton Road. Take another left into Field Lane and a right into Second Field Lane. Continue until you reach Great Field.

2 Take the path in front of you which takes you over the field. (Follow the blue markers). At the other side of the field the path

Braunton Burrows lies at the heart of North Devon's Biosphere Reserve, an accolade awarded by UNESCO (United Nations Educational, Scientific and Cultural Organisation), for its abundance of rare plants and wildlife.

becomes a track which leads you to a road. Turn right and walk along with a stream to your left.

3 At the end of the road take a left onto another road. This leads you down to a car park on your right. Cross the car park, and pick up the path on the other side of a metal gate on which there is a sign: No Unauthorised Vehicles. Leading you towards the dunes the path curves around to the right.

4 Stay on the track until it meets another track and, at this fork, go right. Stay on this path which meanders through the burrows. In summer you'll see wild flowers, colourful beetles, butterflies, mosses and sunbaked lichens as well as bun-

Sand dunes, Braunton Burrows

nies, munching away, creating the distinctive cropped turf. There are many paths through these great sandhills but if you stick to the obvious main track it eventually drops you down onto the beach.

5 Here, with Lundy Island straight ahead, turn right to make a detour to Saunton. Otherwise, turn left and walk with the sea to your right and the dunes to your left

towards Westward Ho! and Appledore. Enjoy this long beach walk until the sand has almost run out.

6 At a cluster of big grey rocks turn left and climb over the remains of a small wooden fence. You are now at Crow Point, a popular spot with bird watchers and fishermen. In front of you is the remnant of what must be one of the most photographed boats in North Devon. Take a left and walk around the edge of the burrows.

Many rare species of bird can be found in the Torridge-Taw Estuary which is noted for its migratory populations of wading birds.

7 Turn left when you come to a path with four large boulders across it and a Military Training Area sign. Then take a right at the path opposite two green information signs. Follow this potholed track which becomes a narrow road. For better views, climb up to the top of the grassy ridge on the right hand side of the road. It runs out at Velator Quay.

Sand dunes, Braunton Burrows

8 At the quay, curve round to your left and join the road. Turn right. Follow the road to the roundabout and turn left. On the other side of the road from the Saltrock Factory Outlet pick up the Tarka Trail.

9 Fluorescent verse lights up the path to your left — poetry for your promenade. At the end of the Tarka Trail take a right then a left. At the police station take a left then a right and pick up the final bit of the Tarka Trail. Turn right into the car park just before the skate park.

Above: Saunton Sands

Below: Crow Point

6 Mortehoe

A 4.5 mile walk on the wild side to Morte Point where dramatic rocks jut out to sea, the cause of many a shipwreck.

'Morte is the place which heaven made last and the devil will take first,' warns the local saying. Treacherous seas, tempestuous weather and a terrifying jagged promontory contribute to its rugged and solitary beauty. Over the centuries many a ship has gone down on the Morte, torn asunder by the razor-like rocks that lie menacingly beneath deceptively balmy blue waters. Few places compare for savage coastal scenery and sheer beauty.

This fairly moderate walk takes you around two of the most dramatic headlands to be found on the North Devon coast. Beginning and ending in Mortehoe, a small hilltop village just north of the popular surfing resort of Woolacombe, it's always an exhilarating experience.

Length: 4.5 miles
Time: 2 hours
Level: 🐾 🐾 Moderate
Directions to get there: Take the A361 from Braunton towards Ilfracombe. Turn left at Mullacott Cross onto the B3343 towards Woolacombe. Take a right at Mortehoe Station Road.
OS Map: OS Landranger 180 Barnstaple and Ilfracombe
Start and park: SS 45800, 45209
Refreshments: The Ship Aground (01271 870856) in Mortehoe serves lunches and evening meals all year around. The Chichester (01271 8704111) in Mortehoe serves lunches and evening meals throughout the summer; Wednesday to Saturday plus Sunday lunch during the winter.
Note: Children need to be supervised on this walk which takes you close to the cliff edge. Whatever the forecast it is advisable to take waterproofs with you. Morte Point seems to have its own unpredictable weather.

Morte Point

Bull Point
Rockham Beach
Lighthouse

④

⑤

Mortehoe 🍴 🚻 🏧

-gate
h

②

⑥

⑦

🚌

North Morte Road

①

Mortehoe Station Road

1 Parking is limited in the little village of Mortehoe so it's best to head for the main car park. Take a left out of the car park entrance and follow the road downhill past the aptly named Ship Aground pub then past The Chichester pub.

2 Pass through a wooden gate on your right and a grassy track will take you downhill. The path soon bears to the right while the sea, if it is a stormy day, will be crashing dramatically onto rocks below you, to your left. If it's gusty there are few paths quite as

bracing. If it's balmy and blue, it can be resplendent. A blaze of colour awaits you in late summer: purple heather offsets yellow gorse and azure waters sparkle in the sun. You may be tempted by various sheep tracks and paths leading off to the right but, if you stick with the lowest level path, it will take you right around the headland directly above waves smacking onto cliffs below. At Windy Cove a backward glance gives you sweeping views of Woolacombe Beach and neighbouring Baggy Point.

3 Morte Slate is the name of the terrifying rock that awaits you at the tip of Morte Point. It's so jagged it looks for all the world as though it was put there just to rip the bowels out of stricken ships. At the tip of the point

View back to Woolacombe

In the early hours of September 24, 1972 at Bull Point, 15 metres of cliff face crashed into the sea and the signal station partly collapsed.

lies a host of razor-like rocks and the currents here are said to be treacherous. In the winter of 1852 five crews met their fate in these waters. Yet on a summer's day, with seaward views out to Lundy Island and a fascinating array of rock formations to marvel at, it's easy to leave maritime history reassuringly in the past. Morte Point, if it's not too windy, is an ideal place to unwrap sandwiches and pour yourself a coffee, a rare chance to picnic on a knife's edge. From this point the path begins to climb upwards.

(4) Eventually you come to a signpost for Bull Point which points you along the coastal path to your left. This path, which takes you up and down, past Whiting and Oreweed Coves and Rockham Bay, popular for its rock pools, leads you directly to Bull Point. If it's been at all wet it can be slippery so, if you want to keep your decorum and avoid your gluteus maximus muscle coming forcefully into contact with the grass, be careful. Keep an eye out for seabirds and, if you are very lucky, you might spot the seemingly-smiley face of a seal bobbing alongside you.

Walkers at Morte Point

Morte Slate at the tip of Morte Point

Morte Point

Bull Point Lighthouse was established in 1879 and operated without undue incident for 93 years.

5 Stocky Bull Point almost makes Morte Point look dainty. Standing guard over its turbulent waters is its equally solid lighthouse. A beam from Bull Point has guided vessels navigating off the North Devon Coast since 1879 helping them avoid the Rockham Shoal and the Morte Stone. At this point, in order to return to Mortehoe, you need to take the tarmac path directly opposite the lighthouse gate, signposted to the village. Lovely coastal views to your right will keep your spirits high.

Above: Bull Point Lighthouse

Below: Tip of Morte Point

Bull Point Lighthouse signal station is now fully automatic and the equipment comes into operation at pre-set times.

6 Pass through a black gate and follow the road. An attractively built stone wall is worth peering over for a wonderful valley view.

7 Go through the metal gates which have written on them 'Bull Point Lighthouse' and follow the main road back into the village. The road returns you to the car park.

7 Arlington

A fairly easy 4.5 mile wildlife walk which includes a visit to Arlington Court, the former home of the eccentric nature lover Miss Chichester.

Rosalie Chichester, the eccentric former owner of Arlington Court, was a free spirit who adored nature. She allowed her pet parrot to fly around the White Drawing Room and her peacocks to come in through the window. Protecting nature was her passion. It's fitting therefore that this countryside walk around Arlington Court, now a National Trust property, is bursting with wildlife. It includes a visit to a hide where you can sit and watch nature's dramas unfold and a stroll through a secluded wooded valley.

Length: 4.5 miles
Time: 2 hours
Level: 🐾 Easy
Directions to get there: From Barnstaple take the A39 towards Lynmouth and follow the signposts to Arlington Court.
OS Map: OS 180 Landranger Barnstaple and Ilfracombe
Start and park: SS 61054 40802
Refreshments: The tea shop at Arlington serves meals.
Note: The walk includes a visit to the Arlington Court, its carriage collection and gardens (for current details on opening times and admission prices, phone 01271 850296). To pay or show your NT membership go through Arlington's main reception and shop.
There are many circular walks around the Arlington Estate and this is just one of the many routes you can take. However, if you are looking for a shorter walk, you can follow signposts back to Arlington Court at several points.

Arlington Court

Stables

1. Opposite the National Trust car park go through Arlington's main reception where you will need to pay an entrance fee (see note above) and follow signs to the circular walk. You'll soon be walking in a stately avenue of Monkey Puzzle trees — these curious trees, sometimes called Chile pine, were all the rage in the 19th century. Follow the wooden signs down to the lake — an attraction created by Sir John Chichester in 1850 by damming the River Yeo.

Arlington Court

2. You'll pass the hide — an ideal viewing point if you enjoy bird watching or have a passion for wildlife photography. Opposite is the heronry — the water birds love to breed near the lake. Inside is a book where people record the animals and birds they've spotted. You might find yourself getting up, close and personal with anything from squirrels to otters. To continue the walk go right, signposted: circular walk. The path takes you along the lake.

3. Once around the lake follow the route signposted: Arlington Court via Smallacombe Bridge and Wilderness. When you get to Smallacombe Bridge take the route signposted: Loxhore and Deerpark Wood.

4 At Tucker's Bridge (written on the sign) take a left sign-posted: Arlington Court and Loxhore via Deerpark Wood.

5 At Deerpark (written on the sign), head straight uphill signposted: Arlington Court via Coombeshead. Keep following signs towards Coombeshead and the track becomes a woodland path. A wooden gate takes you into a field where you may encounter wild Shetland Ponies. (Some of these are descendants of Miss Chichester's ponies — apparently it was a clause in her will that the NT should look after them). Particularly splendid are the white ones which, like hornless unicorns, sometimes race down the hill to greet you. Take a right and climb up the field. There is a

Above: Deerpark Wood, Arlington

As well as being fanatical about wildlife Miss Chichester, an ardent traveller, also loved to collect trinkets, everything from silver spoons to snuff boxes and Arlington Court is full of her treasures.

Below: Bridge, Arlington

Blue Tit at the bird hide, Arlington

A colony of Lesser Horseshoe bats roosts in the roof of Arlington and to see them you can use an interactive bat cam (between May and August).

path which becomes a series of steps nearer the top. Go over the stile at the top, take a left and walk along the fence. The path continues and you will go through a metal gate where you will see a pond in front of you.

6 Continue on the path until you reach a stable block where from each box the long snout of a horse is likely to greet you. Here you need to take a left signposted:

Arlington Court. This farmyard track takes you through a wooden gate, across a field to a gate at the far side of the next field. Go through this gate and follow the hedge. Pass through a small wooden gate taking you into woodland and out through

the gate on the other side. It is not unusual to disturb deer in these woods. (There are yellow footpath signs along this part of the route). Cross this field to the gate opposite which is on the right-hand side of a house.

(7) Climb the stile and take a path which takes you diagonally across the grass towards a barn. You will be able to see Arlington Church from here. At the barn climb over the stile and take a left sign-posted: Arlington Court. Your route will now take you past Arlington's stunning courtyard with its 1864 coach house and stable block, proudly presided over by Peter the peacock. Here your carriage awaits you! The carriage collection houses an overwhelming choice of cabs, chariots and coaches. Not that they'd seriously let you ride in such magnificent antiques of course. However it is fun to dream about which one you'd like to whizz around town in. To continue, follow the path past the church and up to the Regency house itself — a treasure trove of model ships, exotic shells and more. You can also discover the formal gardens and wilderness at your leisure. From the house follow the path back to the car park.

Arlington is a top spot for wildlife and it is not unusual to see rare lichens, dormice, hares, otters, ponies, deer and owls.

Left: Arlington wildlife

Peter the peacock

8 Combe Martin

A fairly hard, 5.9 mile, mostly uphill climb which is rewarded by incredible views at the top of two of North Devon's finest coastal peaks.

Hungry for sumptuous views? The two summits in this walk around Combe Martin give you plenty to feast your eyes on. Neighbouring coastal peaks, Great Hangman and Little Hangman, offer some of the most delicious 360 degree panoramas in the South West. Admittedly the first three miles of this walk are an uphill climb but the visual rewards certainly justify the exertion. Work up an appetite then banquet on your sandwiches and two of the most outstanding outlooks in the region.

Length: 5.9 miles
Time: 2 hours 30 mins
Level: ♥♥♥ Hard. Although this is a short walk the first three miles are a continuous climb
Directions to get there: Take the A361 to Ilfracombe and then the A399 to Combe Martin. Parade Car Park is on your left as you get to the harbour.
OS Map: Landranger 180 Barnstaple and Ilfracombe
Start and park: SS 57569 47268
Refreshments: Combe Martin has a wide selection of pubs and eateries to choose from.

ATLANTIC OCEAN

Wild Pear Beach

7 Little Hangman

6 Great Hangman

EXMOOR NATIONAL PARK

5

Combe Martin

3

Farm Buildings

4

Pack o' Cards

2

Watery Lane

1 The walk starts at Parade Car Park which, as car parks go, has to boast one of the best aspects, overlooking Combe Martin beach as it does. Looking out to sea, take the path that leads to the right in the direction of the beach. This then joins Combe Martin's main street (which, claiming to be longest village street in the UK, at just over two miles, seems

The Pack O' Cards pub was built by George Ley in 1626 after a big win at cards. Consequently it has 52 windows (one for each card in the pack), four floors (one for each suit), and 13 doors on each floor (one for each card in the suit).

to enjoy a variety of names). Follow the main road through the seaside village, once famous for its strawberries and silver mining. This takes you past the harbour and the tourist shops into more residential parts. Eventually you'll come to the curiously-shaped Pack O' Cards on your right.

2 Take the next turning left into Chapel Lane, narrowly squeezed between the Post Office and the Baptist Chapel. Ignoring any avenues going off to the side, follow this lane right up to the top. Turn left into Watery Lane, a path between high hedges which, due to a little stream that trickles down here if it has been raining, can be wet underfoot. The path goes across a couple of tracks but you need to continue fol-

Pack O' Cards

lowing the yellow footpath signs to the top.

3 At the narrow road turn right signposted: Footpath to Great Hangman Via Knap Down Lane. There is a seat quite soon on your right and it is great vantage point. Take the next left signposted: Great Hangman Knap Down Lane. Stay on this path which gradually climbs. Don't forget to glance behind you for ever improving views. When the path flattens you'll see undulating green fields to your left.

(4) At the end of this path take a left signposted: Great Hangman. Follow this farm lane down-hill and just before the house turn right through a metal gate followed by a wooden gate. It is sign-posted: Great Hangman. Go past the farm buildings and the path swings around to the left. Go through a couple of wooden gates and bear right across a field to a wooden gate oppo-site. Climb over the stile next to the gate which is marked by the National Trust sign: Great Hangman. The path follows a wall on your right and crosses a grassy area.

View to sea from Little Hangman

(5) At the grassy crossroads turn left following the coast path sign. In the late summer this stretch of path is ablaze with heather and gorse. You are now climbing Great Hangman.

(6) At the summit, 1043 ft, marked by a pile of stones, you will be rewarded with an astounding view. It's quiet here, a perfect place for a picnic. Look out to

Little Hangman

The Hunting of the Earl of Rone has livened up many a May in Combe Martin: a traditional pagan hobby horse procession in which the Earl is pursued, mounted the wrong way around on a donkey before being ceremoniously dumped in the sea.

sea: behind you are undulating fields, to your right heather-clad Holdstone Down, in front of you the Welsh coastline and to your left Little Hangman in the foreground, with cliffs, coves and Lundy Island stretching into the distance. It doesn't get much better than this — well until you get to the summit of Little Hangman that is! The

path descends the other side. Go through the gate in the little stone wall and keep following the path down as it leads you all the way along the coast.

7 You pass Little Hangman — do take the detour to the summit. It's not to be missed. Point

your camera in any direction and the views are outstanding. On a clear day Wales looks like a nearby headland. Go down the same way you came up and the path continues to descend taking you around the top of Wild Pear Beach and through a gate. Take the path straight in front of you signposted: Coast Path Combe Martin. This

View from Great Hangman

View across Combe Martin Bay

Above: Views at Hangman, Combe Martin   Below: Wind bent trees, Exmoor

climbs a little bit before descending into the town. You need to take a right at the fork just after the shelter. Soon, above Combe Martin harbour, you come to a steep grassy area which you need to go down. At the bottom turn left into a row of parking spaces leading you into Kiln Car Park. Go through the car park and, with the Tourist Information building to your left, turn right and follow the road which swings around to the left into Cross Street. Turn right onto the main road which leads you up to the car park on your right.

Hemp used to be grown in the village and large quantities of shoe makers' thread spun from it.

9 Weare Giffard

A fairly flat and easy, 6.9 mile walk meandering through the heart of Tarka Country and the pretty inland village of Weare Giffard.

No North Devon walk book would be complete without a visit to the birthplace of its most eminent otter. The River Torridge has one of the healthiest populations of these waterside wanderers in the UK and is most famous, of course, as the fictional birthplace of Tarka The Otter from Henry Williamson's 1927 book of the same name. This walk takes you along the Tarka Trail, a fabulous walking and cycling track, which follows the course of the old railway that once ran from Barnstaple to the south of Torrington. It also leads you through the pretty meandering village of Weare Giffard.

Length: 6.9 miles

Time: 2 hours 15 mins

Level: Easy. This is a relatively flat walk with just has a few short climbs on Torrington Commons.

OS Map: Landranger 180 Barnstaple and Ilfracombe

Start and park: SS 48015 19748

Refreshments: The Puffing Billy (01805 623050) at Torrington serves refreshments but is worth calling for opening hours as these can be weather dependent. The Cyder Presse (01237 425517) Weare Giffard is open for lunches and evening meals all year around with longer opening hours in the school holidays.

Note: The Tarka Trail is suitable for pushchairs, wheelchairs and bicycles and makes for a fun day out for all the family in its own right. As an alternative to this circular walk park at the Puffing Billy and follow the Tarka Trail along to Beam Weir and back.

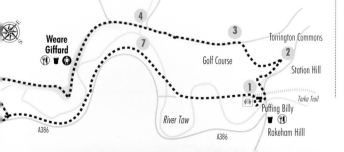

① The walk starts at the Puffing Billy pub, a former railway station, which houses a collection of old photos from the heyday of the railway (you might also meet resident parrots Tilly and Victor). From the Puffing Billy car park go out to the road and turn left and cross over a bridge which arches over the Tarka Trail. On the other side, just past a private drive, take a path on the left. This immediately forks and you need to take a left (you don't want Alexanda Path). The path soon meets another path and, at this fork, turn left again. Go across the flat stone bridge which takes you across the stream and turn right. You will pass a stone called Barmaid's Path on your left. This path takes you up through the bracken, gorse and pretty wild flowers of Torrington Commons.

Tarka Trail

This stretch of the Tarka Trail was built on the old railway line which in turn followed the course of the old Rolle Canal, carrying coal and limestone from the port of Bideford to Torrington.

Weare Giffard village green

2 At the fork take the grassy path to the left. You soon come to a wide track. Turn left here and climb uphill. Soon you will find yourself passing the golf course to your left.

3 The path leads you alongside the golf course and eventually comes out at a road. Turn left here and a country lane takes you all the way into Weare Giffard.

4 Follow the main road which meanders for a mile or so through this mix of modern houses and traditional cottages, eventually leading you past Weare Giffard Hall, an extremely impressive old manor house, and the village church which is worth a visit. You'll then pass a farm on your left.

Cottage in Weare Giffard

5 At the junction by the Weare Giffard sign take a left, sign-posted: Bideford and Monkleigh. Go over the bridge and you'll pass Avery Kiln on your right. Go under a bridge and follow the road that curves around to your right.

6 At Weare Giffard Cross, just before the main road, take a right through a gap in a wooden gate. You are now on the Tarka Trail. Turn right.

7 Enjoy this attractive stretch of the Tarka Trail which leads you back to the Puffing Billy. Depending on the time of year you'll find yourself walking beneath a leafy green canopy as branches from the tree-lined path meet overhead.

Bridge near Avery Kiln, Weare Giffard

In summer the banks are full of wild flowers including dog rose, cow parsley and herb Robert and in spring they are adorned with primroses. Look out for good views of Weare Giffard through the trees to your left.

Who might you meet here? Well at dusk or nightfall in the warmer months you might encounter the odd bat or two – it's a good feeding ground for these nocturnal creatures. If you are extremely lucky, where the track crosses the river at Beam Weir

Thatched cottage, Weare Giffard

you might spot a family of otters. It's worth a little wait and a quiet watch — even a glimpse of these five-toed creatures is a great thrill.

You might witness the odd leaping salmon too, completing the final stage of its return journey to spawn. And, if you are imaginative enough, you might like to conjure up the image of Tarka The Otter playing by the oaks close to Canal Bridge. This is his fictional birthplace which can be seen from the Tarka Trail.

In the late evening you sometimes hear otters whistling along the River Torridge — usually a courting pair or a mum calling her pups.

Fly fishing, River Torridge

10 Baggy Point

A popular and attractive 7 mile beach walk which leads you from the charming thatches of Croyde to the surfing resort of Woolacombe.

Croyde, they say, got its name from a Viking raider called Crydda but there's not much evidence of pillaging and plundering in the popular surfing hotspot these days. Instead the little cluster of cottages and shops at the heart of the village has a classic Devon charm — think thatched roofs, window boxes and cream teas.

If you fancy a day out on the coast, this walk offers you a romantic roam around a windswept headland, a stroll along a long stretch of golden sands followed by a gentle drift through the dunes. Remarkably, despite only being a stone's throw from the holidaying hordes of Croyde, at Baggy Point it feels as though time stands still.

Length: 7 miles
Time: 3 hours
Level: Moderate. Although this is a long walk, an alternative route is given for those seeking a shorter stroll — see marker 5. It is also possible to skip the stretch that takes you along the beach from Putsborough to Woolacombe. In this case once you have reached the end of the coastal path at Putsborough you need to continue with marker 8 below. Reference to the OS map is recommended.

Directions to get there: From Braunton take the B3231 to Croyde and then turn left onto Jones's Hill then turn left into Moor Lane and follow to the NT Baggy Point Car Park.

OS Map: Landranger 180 Barnstaple and Ilfracombe

Start and park: SS 43222 39691

Refreshments: There are plenty of eateries in Croyde. In Woolacombe the Red Barn, popular with families and surfers, serves bar meals all day.

1. From the NT car park take a right. Ignore the private road to Croyde Hoe Farm and stay on the lower path which gradually curves around the headland. Soon you'll pass a curiosity to your right – a large whale, washed up on Croyde beach in 1915. By walkers' standards you'll find the track, which leads you to the craggy headland of Baggy Point, pretty excellent. A popular path with families, you even see people pushing children's buggies along here.

Cliffs, Baggy Point

2. Baggy Point itself is a fabulous viewing point – a dramatic rocky promontory with stunning sea views. In one eyeful you can drink in sweeping vistas across Bideford Bay to Hartland Point, while imposing cliffs demonstrate the power of the sea to create its own awe-inspiring architecture.

Watch the white waves smash into the weather-wrinkled cliffs – it looks for all the world as if someone has deliberately and painstakingly chiseled

View towards Croyde from Baggy Point

Baggy Point, famous for its geological features and rugged cliffs is within a Site of Special Scientific Interest.

fancy geometrical patterns into them. The point's sheer shale also makes it a popular hangout (excuse the pun) with climbers.

(3) From here onwards the terrain becomes more challenging. The path leads you upwards from Baggy Point to a wooden gate. Go through it and turn left, following the path around the edge of the field, with the sea to your left. At the top you'll want to take in the view: in the distance you see the beautiful stretch of sands between Putsborough and Woolacombe, flanked by Morte Point. You may be tempted to follow one of the well-worn sheep tracks – don't. These take you perilously near the edge. Instead, stay on the main path which takes you past a white post.

(4) You'll pass a wall to your right which is worth peeping over for views back to Croyde.

(5) Eventually you come to a NT signpost. If you are weary take a right here and it will lead you back to the car park. If you want more

Dunes at Woolacombe

Baggy Point

Towards Putsborough from Baggy Point

of a challenge stay on the gorse-laden path that now descends to Putsborough.

(6) Follow the path to the end where you can turn left onto a road taking you down to

The Hyde family, keen to preserve its beauty, gave Baggy Point to the National Trust in 1939.

Putsborough car park. From here climb down onto the beach and turn right. Enjoy this long stretch of sands which, if you have the energy, will take you all the way to the seaside resort of Woolacombe.

(7) There are several ways to pick up the path that leads through the dunes and back to Putsborough. Here's one: walk along the beach in the direction of Putsborough until you come to a big cluster of grey rocks. At this point clamber up from the sands and follow the path into the dunes, turning right. The main track, that runs parallel to the sea, leads you all the way back to Putsborough beach. Clamber down to the sands again at the other end.

Rainbow over Putsborough

(8) Take the tarmac road leading up from Putsborough car park and at the top turn right onto the road.

(9) Continue until you come to a big metal gate on your right

and a coast path sign. Go over the stile at the side of the gate and continue along the grass track.

(10) When the wall to your left runs out, a yellow arrow points you across the field to the far left hand

corner. You might be able to see a track across the field taking you there.

(11) Climb the stone stile which drops you down onto a sunken path, following yellow foot-path signs. When the sunken path comes to an end turn right. You will be walking on a track between two high hedges. Stay on this. After a while it swings to the left and you cross over a stile. The path narrows and then takes you over a row of

Croyde has an eccentric local tradition: carousing men falling into the village stream get crowned Mayor of Croyde, a title they keep until the next drunken buffoon gets a soaking.

bricks on top of a stream. Keep an eye out for overhanging branches and the odd wobbly brick under foot.

(12) At the end of the bricks turn left. This track takes you all

the way back to the road.

(13) At the road take a right and Baggy Point car park will soon appear on your right.

View across Woolacombe Beach